how2become

How to Become an
Australian Police Officer

www.How2Become.com

As part of this product you have also received FREE access to online tests that will help you to become a Police Officer.

To gain access, simply go to:

www.MyPsychometricTests.co.uk

Get more products for passing any test at:

www.How2Become.com

Introduction

Many young people aspire to become members of Australia's police forces. While aspirations are one thing, successfully completing the application process and the selection process are quite another.

Not everyone is suited to the role of a police officer. Often, a police officer will have to put the safety of others before the safety of themselves, and they must always bear the public's interest and wellbeing in mind. Police officers need to be physically, morally and psychologically fit in order to perform their job properly. For this reason, the selection process is incredibly stringent and will ask a lot of any candidate who wishes to apply. Applying to become a police officer, or indeed becoming one, is not for the faint of heart. Bear this in mind before starting your application.

Having said this, do not let the challenge put you off your dream career. Joining any worthwhile police service will be difficult, but the benefits of being a police officer are tremendous. The training is tough but rewarding, and a whole world of career opportunities can open up once you have completed the selection process. Additionally, police officers work alongside likeminded individuals in an environment which demands mutual respect between colleagues. It's also a career that pays well and offers a lot of holiday and leave time, respecting the work-life balance of officers.

Whether you are interested in a career with the Australian Federal Police (AFP), or if you aspire to become a sheriff's officer, bailiff, or a member of a certain state's police force, you must first meet several minimum requirements. These include having a valid driver's license and a first-aid certificate. The minimum requirements for becoming a police officer in Australia are detailed in chapter 2.

You must then complete an application that will be reviewed prior to the selection process. The application is only the first step of many that lead successful candidates to careers within Australia's finest police forces; taking the time to fill it out thoughtfully and thoroughly is absolutely vital if you hope to move forward with the selection process. Details on passing the application stage can be found in chapter 3.

During the selection process itself, you will submit to a number of

Disclaimer

Every effort has been made to ensure that the information contained within this guide is accurate at the time of publication. How2Become Ltd is not responsible for anyone failing any part of any selection process as a result of the information contained within this guide. How2Become Ltd and their authors cannot accept any responsibility for any errors or omissions within this guide, however caused. No responsibility for loss or damage occasioned by any person acting, or refraining from action, as a result of the material in this publication can be accepted by How2Become Ltd. The information within this guide does not represent the views of any third party service or organisation.

Orders: Please contact How2Become Ltd, Suite 14, 50 Churchill Square Business Centre, Kings Hill, Kent ME19 4YU.

You can order through Amazon.co.uk under ISBN: 9781912370092, via the website www.How2Become.com or through Ingram.

ISBN: 9781912370092

First published in 2018 by How2Become Ltd.

Typeset by Gemma Butler for How2Become Ltd.

Contents

- Probing Questions

- Verifying Questions

- Hypothetical Questions

- Sample Questions and Answers

- Australian Law Enforcement Agency Information

- Pre-Employment Education

tests that are specifically designed to assess your mental, physical, and emotional capacities. If you pass those tests successfully, you will move forward to the interview process. Information on these tests can be found in chapters 4 and 5.

Candidates who make it to the interview stage will be asked a series of questions to get a better understanding of yourself in person. By this point, your potential employers probably have a general idea with regards to your physical and mental aptitude, as well as your beliefs and attitudes. The interview stage is a candidate's chance to back up their performance with great interpersonal skills. More information about the interview, as well as some sample questions, can be found in chapter 7.

Before continuing to look at the application process, it is important that you learn how the different police services in Australia operate. While you might not be tested on the history of these forces, it is helpful to know their stories since it will round out your knowledge, and perhaps draw you to a specific service. Hopefully you will also find it interesting to learn about the history of policing in Australia.

Chapter 1
The Roles of
Australia's
Police Officers

Throughout Australia, law enforcement is facilitated by a number of different bodies including police, bailiffs, and sheriffs. Additionally, there are a few agencies which specialise in white-collar crime, such as money laundering, embezzlement and racketeering. Each agency is responsible for enforcing the laws within the boundaries of its jurisdiction. For instance, the police are primarily responsible for the enforcement of criminal laws, whilst the sheriff's officers and bailiffs of each state enforce civil law.

Each state has its own police force, which is responsible for the enforcement of state laws and city statutes, while the Australian Federal Police are responsible for investigating any crimes against Commonwealth laws as well as for community policing in conjunction with local agencies. All agencies co-operate with one another, occasionally transferring cases between one another, depending on existing circumstances.

Australian Federal Police (AFP)

The Australian Federal Police, or AFP, is an international law enforcement agency tasked with enforcing criminal law within the Commonwealth of Australia and protecting its interests overseas. Formed on 19 October 1979, it merged the former Commonwealth Police, the Australian Capital Territory Police, and the Federal Bureau of Narcotics. It is held within the portfolio of the Home Affairs Ministry, with its key priorities being set by the Australian Minister for Home Affairs.

The AFP provides community police services to the Australian Capital Territory, the Jervis Bay Territory, Christmas Island, Norfolk Island, the Cocos Islands, and it maintains an extensive international liaison network, with officers occupying 33 different international posts. Consisting of a workforce of more than 6,500 individuals, the AFP focuses on illicit drug trafficking, human trafficking, fraud against the government, organised crime, money laundering, and high-tech crime. In addition, the AFP prevents, counters, and investigates acts of terrorism. Keeping the peace and preserving public safety are top priorities.

The AFP is also home to the Specialist Response Group, an elite unit focused on providing tactical solutions to high and critical risk incidents. This includes disaster response, restoration of law and order, and bomb response.

The AFP also maintains a world-renowned Ceremonial Team, which includes the AFP Ceremonial Mounted Cadre and the AFP Pipes and Drums, which perform ceremonial duties at a number of functions and ceremonies.

State Police

Each state within the Commonwealth is responsible for maintaining its own police force, as is the Northern Territory. State Police are responsible for maintaining law and order and handling traffic incidents and accidents, as well as for handling crimes. Water Police, Search and Rescue personnel, and anti-terrorism experts are some of the specialists who are employed by various State Police agencies. In some states, local governments employ additional officers called By-Laws Officers to handle matters such as parking, dog ownership, retailing, and other specific laws and ordinances. Many By-Laws police are appointed as Special Constables or have been granted authority by local legislators.

State Police perform many functions on behalf of the Australian government, including enforcement of Commonwealth Acts and Regulations. In sparsely populated areas, they also handle Sheriff's duties.

New South Wales Police Force

Formed in 1862 after the passing of the Police Regulation Act, the NSW Police Force is the longest-standing and currently the largest police force in Australia. It merged with the NSW Police Department as a result of the Police Act of 1990, making the NSW Police Force of today.

With just under 17,000 staff and over 500 police stations, the NSW Police Force is more than a noteworthy part of Australia's police force. It serves seven million civilians over 801,000 square kilometres of land, making it one of the biggest police forces in the English-speaking world.

Northern Territory Police
Policing in the Northern Territory has existed since 1870, but the Northern Territory Police known today was founded in 1911. In the past fifty years, the number of police officers operating in the Northern Territory Police has grown from less than one hundred to over 1,300. It serves a population of 229,000 over a vast 1.3 million square kilometres and is host to a number of specialist groups.

Queensland Police
Queensland State broke away from New South Wales in 1859, and founded its first police force in 1864.It began with less than 150 employees, but by 2012 it would employ over 15,000 staff, 10,000 of which are police officers. Based in Brisbane, the Queensland Police Force became the Queensland Police Service and serves five different regions in Queensland.

South Australia Police
The South Australia Police was formed in 1838, making it the oldest police force in Australia and among the oldest police services in the world. With 138 stations across over 1 million square kilometres, the 5000 officers serve a population of approximately 1.7 million people.

Tasmania Police
With a jurisdiction of almost 70,000 square kilometres and serving 500,000 people, the Tasmania Police is relatively small compared to other police services and jurisdictions in Australia. Tasmania's police service employs approximately 1,600 people, including 1,200 officers.

Victoria Police
Established in 1853, Victoria Police currently serves almost 6 million Australians in Victoria State. It has over 14,000 sworn officers, as well as almost 3,000 civilian staff operating in 329 police stations. Community confidence in Victoria Police is very high, with over

75% of Victorians being satisfied with their police service.

Western Australia Police
West Australia Police was formally founded in 1853 when a Chief of Police was assigned to what was once a troop of mounted police. Today, it covers 2.5 million square kilometres of land, serving a population of 2.5 million with over 120 police stations. The Western Australia Police currently employs over 6,000 sworn officers as well as over 2,500 administrative staff.

Sheriffs and Bailiffs

Sheriffs and Bailiffs are primarily responsible for recovering court ordered fines. However, sheriffs' and bailiffs' duties are not consistent throughout the states. Each state defines specific roles for employees of these departments. In the past, these departments were responsible for managing the gaols (jails), transporting prisoners, acting as coroners, and carrying out executions. Today, the departments deal primarily with the court system. Some common duties include:

- Maintaining court security;

- Seizing and selling the property of judgment debtors;

- Enforcing arrest warrants;

- Taking juveniles into custody;

- Handling evictions when necessary.

In some states, Sheriffs are also responsible for enforcing drivers' licensing laws and auto registration laws, arranging for community service, and making arrests.

Council Rangers

Often referred to as 'Local Laws Officers', Council Rangers under the command of Local Government Areas to enforce the by-laws of those bodies, as well as to enforce certain state laws. Unless they are sworn as Special Constables, Council Rangers do not have full police powers. Often tasked with fire control, emergency management, enforcing off-road vehicle laws and dog ownership laws, their job description varies greatly from one local area to the next.

Other Police Agencies

A number of other police agencies are tasked with the enforcement of various laws and mandates; some of these agencies include regulatory agencies such as the Australian Fisheries Management Authority (AFMA) amongst others. In recent years, many of these agencies have merged into larger departments, but a few specialised groups still exist. There are also multiple Defence law enforcement agencies, including the Defence Security Authority (DSA), the Australian Defence Force Investigative Service (ADFIS), and the Royal Australian Corps of Military Police (RACMP).

What it takes the become a Police Officer in Australia

So far, we have discussed the different state police services as well as the federal agencies recruiting in Australia. From the descriptions given, you might already have an idea of which police service (or services) you would like to work for.

While these agencies and forces may have slightly different focuses based on their expertise and location, all of them work towards the same goal of reducing crime and protecting civilians. Of course, this goal can manifest in multiple ways: a bailiff enforcing traffic laws and a counter-terror unit have vastly different training and experience, but are both working to enforce the law and protect people. Bear this in mind when making your application.

Chapter 2
The Application
Process

When applying for any new job, it is of utmost importance to complete the application process correctly. When applying for a job as a police officer, the application holds an incredible amount of weight. Your ability to move through the rest of the selection process is determined by your ability to complete the application properly. Not only should you have a thorough understanding of the qualities candidates must possess to successfully carry out the role of Police Officer, you must meet some specific minimum requirements.

Minimum Requirements

If you want to become a police officer in Australia, you must:

*   Be over the age of 18;

*   Have competed either Year 12 education or Year 10 with a trade certificate or similar qualification;

*   Be an Australian citizen or New Zealand Citizen with a special category visa;

*   Have a valid manual vehicle driver's licence;

*   Be healthy and physically fit;

*   Be self-motivated and willing to serve;

*   Have a first-aid certificate;

*   Have the confirmed ability to swim 100 metres freestyle, non-stop, clothed and unaided.

Some police departments have additional requirements. Before applying to any police department, it is advisable to learn which physical, educational, and other requirements applicants must possess. These details are readily accessible on each service's website.

Desirable Candidate Qualities

No matter which department you hope to apply for, you should be aware that all Australian police agencies look for the very best candidates possible. The testing and selection process are designed to weed out those candidates who do not meet minimum physical, mental, and emotional standards; candidates who excel in certain categories are understandably much more desirable than those who do not. Some desirable qualities for those who wish to take on the role of Police Officer include the following:

- Honesty, personal accountability, and integrity. Candidates will undergo thorough background investigations to ensure that they meet the standards of the service.

- A clean record. While people with minor criminal convictions and traffic convictions are welcome to apply for positions, some convictions are serious enough to prevent an applicant from moving forward. If you have a conviction on your record, you should discuss it openly with recruitment personnel to find out whether it would affect your chances of successful selection.

- Extra education or work experience. Prior learning experience such as college credit will help your chances. In addition, if you have had some previous work experience, particularly work within some capacity of law enforcement, your chances of success improve. Whilst police departments offer academy training, some applicants are more desirable due to their maturity and past experiences. If you do not have any of these extra experiences, it may be worth applying for some relevant courses or work experience before applying for a police officer role.

- Undertaking and passing medical and drugs tests. Prior to engagement, all successful applicants are required to undergo final medical examinations and testing for illicit drugs, along with a final security clearance. Maintaining a drug-free lifestyle and becoming as physically fit as possible is advisable.

Australia's police forces are committed to recruiting individuals from all of the diverse groups that make up Australian society. Your gender, ethnicity, race, sexual preference or other differences do not place you at any disadvantage.

How and Where to Apply

Applying for a Police Officer position isn't overly difficult, but there a number of things to consider before jumping in. First, you must decide which police department you wish to apply to. Some candidates place applications with multiple departments in order to speed up the process. This is a lot more work at the start of the process, but having a number of applications processing at once can be more time-efficient than applying for positions once at a time.

Before choosing a department or service to apply to, take some time to research what that department does. What areas do its officers work in? Where are officers stationed? What are their duty schedules like? What opportunities for advancement does the department offer? Many police departments offer career information sessions that can help make the decision making process easier.

Putting serious thought into the application process not only helps you make an educated decision about which department or departments to apply to, it also shows recruitment personnel within those departments that you are serious about your commitment to put forth your best effort during the application, selection, and training process. Taking the time to seriously consider which departments suit your personality and goals will show interviewers that you want the job. Ultimately, departments choose the candidates that are most likely to succeed; these are often the candidates who show the most personal initiative from the outset.

Once you have decided to begin the application process with a specific police department, you can begin your application. Many police departments offer online applications, and most departments have personnel specifically dedicated to recruiting new members. You may pick up an application at a jobs or career event, or you may simply print it out at home.

Be sure you know when and where to turn in your application. Applications completed online may be submitted online; some departments may ask you to submit your application in person. Other departments may request candidates submit their application by mail. In any case, double-check the requirements for sending in your application since it's the first step to your dream career.

Tips for Completing the Application Form

Unless you are completing your application online, make a few extra copies of your application. The reason for this is that you need to turn in an absolutely spotless copy to make a good first impression. Work on your application in a clean environment, away from anything that might spill on it, and ensure that there are no distractions as you begin the process of filling out required forms.

If you're completing online applications, keep multiple copies of any documents you need, preferably on multiple devices. Backing up your C.V. and any other application materials onto a USB drive means that if anything happens to your original copy, you still have another saved and ready to go.

Before beginning, take the time to read each of the questions carefully. Make a list of materials you might need to complete some areas of the application, such as:

- Your driving licence;

- Your birth certificate or other citizenship documents;

- Accurate information about previous employment dates and locations;

- Accurate information regarding education, including locales and dates;

- A list of trustworthy personal references including neighbours, friends, and relations.

The information different departments ask for varies. Before beginning, be sure you have everything you need. Being prepared before starting is just the first step to filling out an application that will appeal to the police staff assigned to accepting or rejecting candidates.

Additionally, make sure that your application is well-presented and easy to follow. The staff assigned to reviewing applications will appreciate it if yours is organised, and might make you a preferable candidate in the process. After all, if they have trouble reading and understanding your application, a potential employer is less likely to see your qualities and therefore is less likely to offer you a job. For this reason, it is absolutely vital that you spend time making sure that all of your documents and materials are well-organised for your application.

In this chapter, you have learned the basics for filling in an application, such as the minimum requirements, desirable qualities and how to apply. In the next chapter, you will be familiarised with the top ten tips for sending off a successful application and making sure it stands out from the crowd.

Chapter 3
Ten Vital Tips
for a Successful
Application

Before filling out your application, ensure you have gathered all necessary materials as outlined in chapter two, and as required by the department for which you are applying. If you are applying for a position within more than one law enforcement agency, be sure that you have everything you need for completing all applications. Prepare in advance to take the stress out of the application process. Use the following tips and guidelines to craft an excellent application.

Schedule a Time and Place for Completing Applications

Just as you would with any other vital task, set aside a precise time and place for completing police applications. Be sure that you are well-rested before you begin, and ensure that you are comfortable; being well hydrated and well-nourished can affect your performance. This may seem excessive, but being focused while writing your application will help you avoid silly mistakes such as misspellings and anything else which may cause confusion.

Police agencies use initial applications as a method for selecting the best candidates. Being at your best when you complete applications will ensure that you do the best you can, and it will make your application stand head and shoulders above applications from others who have never received or failed to follow this advice.

Read and Follow All Instructions Carefully

Before you touch pen to paper, be sure you have read all of the instructions given to you by the department you are applying to. This is important for two reasons. Firstly, failing to follow a vital instruction could make your application void. For example, a department might require two photocopies of the same document in order to process your application properly. If a candidate failed to supply an extra photocopy, then the department would not be able to continue the application.

Secondly, failing to follow an instruction might not prevent the application from continuing, but may make it more difficult to process it. If this happens, all you are doing is showing that you have been unable to read the instructions carefully, which could impact your chances of success. Remember that you are applying to become a police officer, and with that comes the expectation that you are able to pay close attention to detail as well as recognise and follow instructions. Failing to show this during the application process will not bode well for your application.

Once you have read the instructions, read all of the questions. Some questions may seem like duplicates, but you'll notice that they are in fact different from one another. Before writing or typing anything, consider your answers carefully. Remember, you are going to be judged on your answers so they need to be as clear and concise as possible. Before writing anything into your application, jot down some notes on some scrap paper so that you can gather your thoughts. Remember not to hand these notes in with your application.

If you are going in-person to fill out an application, bring high quality blue and black ink pens with you. Some departments ask applicants to use blue ink, whilst others prefer applicants to use black ink. Simply using the wrong type of ink can cause recruitment personnel to reject an application. As previously mentioned, this is because departments want candidates which can take note of instructions and follow them to the letter. Bring extra pens in case you run out of ink, and be sure the pens are of the same brand. Going the extra mile to ensure your application has a streamlined look will help to get you noticed.

Select References Carefully

Before going to fill out an application, or before working on an application at home, be sure that you have selected a number of people to serve as personal references for you.

Ask in advance before using someone as a reference, and tell them that you plan to provide police recruiters with their names, telephone numbers, addresses, and e-mail addresses. If a person seems uncomfortable with this, find someone else to use as a reference.

Be sure you tell everyone you know that you plan to apply for work within the police force. If your application is selected and you move forward with testing, you will at some point be put through a complete background investigation for security purposes. Police detectives assigned to conduct background checks on applicants are thorough, often seeking childhood friends, old neighbours, and distant relations to quiz about the way the applicant conducted himself or herself throughout life. Making sure that your acquaintances, friends and relatives are aware of this might be helpful.

Never Bend the Truth

Do not, under any circumstances, lie on your application. Do not bend the truth, not even a little bit. Police officers are human beings. They have often made mistakes in their lives. Some of them may have made the same kind of mistakes that you have made before they were police officers.

Police recruiters and background investigators know that teenagers often drink while underage or experiment with drugs. Most people have received some kind of traffic ticket in the past, or have been reprimanded for minor misdemeanours. Errors are part of being human. So long as you learned from your mistakes, paid fines, or took other action as necessary to correct your behaviour, you should be fine.

So, if an application asks whether you have tried marijuana, and the answer is "yes", be sure to answer truthfully. Be honest about answering follow-up questions, such as "When was the last time you used marijuana?" "How often did you use marijuana?" Do not try to cover up the truth about your past. Police services cannot tolerate dishonesty since officers have such a huge responsibility in society. Therefore, you must not lie or bend the truth during any part of your application. If you did lie, and the truth came out, there could be severe consequences. Being honest from the start is essential.

Be Prepared to Explain Answers

Be prepared to answer questions about your background, and be ready to provide honest answers to explain past behaviour and to explain the ways in which you have changed, if applicable. In some cases, you might fill out an application one day and be contacted by a background investigator the next. Being completely honest and open in answering inquiries

Be prepared to be consistent. Investigators look for inconsistencies as a method for weeding out undesirable candidates. Be sure names, dates, and other information is correct on your application, and keep information with you so that you can provide follow-up answers if necessary.

Police agencies are now checking social media sites to see what applicants have posted in the past, and some things that you deleted might still be accessible to background officers. Be ready to answer questions about your social media activity.

Avoid Common Mistakes

There are a number of common mistakes people make when turning in police applications. Avoiding these mistakes can help make your application shine.

- Don't cross anything out, and do not scribble, either. This is why you should get at least two copies of the application; get at least one for practice, and complete a perfect copy to turn in. Writing your answers down on note paper before writing them properly on the application can help avoid this mistake.

- Do not leave any spaces blank. If something does not apply to you, write "Not Applicable" or "N/A".

- If writing an application by hand, complete it neatly. Many police agencies have applicants complete forms by hand so that they can see how your handwriting looks. Do not write in script; write in print instead. Strive for a neat and consistent style.

- Do not work too fast. Focus on what you are doing, and shut out any distractions. Despite the fact that this is a relatively simple task, it needs to be done perfectly.

- If there are essay questions, be sure to think carefully before providing an answer. Some essay questions have more than one answer block to complete; reading the application before beginning can help you to complete each block correctly.

- When completing applications online, be sure that you click all submission buttons carefully and ensure you save any confirmation information that pops up. In addition, consider saving your answers on a separate document so you can re-submit with ease, if necessary.

- If mailing your application, ensure the envelope you use looks just as good as the application it contains.

Check Your Spelling and Punctuation

Proofreading work can often feel like a chore, and sometimes it can be painful to read over what you've written. However, it's likely that you've probably made a mistake somewhere in your application, and proofreading your work will allow you to pinpoint any errors in your work.

Some of us just need a little extra help in the spelling and punctuation department. If you know for a fact that your writing skills are not quite up to par, consider taking a remedial course before you even apply to work with a police department. A big part of the job of police officer is to write detailed reports about incidents, accidents, and crimes. Spelling and punctuation are vital skills for success in fieldwork, just as they are for desk jobs.

If possible, give your application to a trusted friend or family member, and ask that person to look for errors. Often, a fresh pair of eyes can spot errors you've missed; having those eyes belong to a friend or relative is much better than allowing police personnel to find your mistakes. This way, you can spot and correct any errors or ambiguities in your application.

If you are filling out a physical application (i.e. on paper), then re-write the entire application if you find mistakes. The effort will pay off in the end. Remember to continue to focus on turning in a quality copy, even if you are writing information for a third or fourth time.

Ensure You Attach Any Required Documentation Correctly

Many police agencies require candidates to turn in additional documentation with their applications. Some ask that additional pages be stapled to the application, while others ask applicants to use paper clips or place all documentation in a certain type of folder. Do not neglect these requirements.

In addition, be sure any copies you turn in are of good quality. If your copier at home is not the best, go to an office centre and pay a small fee to make good copies. Ensure documents have straight, clean edges, and check that they are completely readable. Again, if you are unsure whether they are easy to read, have a family member or friend look at your application to see if anything needs to be printed again. A second set of eyes will spot any documents which are difficult to read.

Double check to ensure you include all necessary documentation. Take a few minutes to make sure that you have every document necessary for the application, including extra copies if required. The easier you make recruiters' jobs, the better your chances of success. Don't just tell them why you're a great candidate, do all you can to prove it.

Turn Your Application In On Time

Often, police departments accept applications during specific time periods. If you hope to gain employment during a specific time span, then be sure you know when the deadline for turning in applications is. If you're applying and it's close to the end of one hiring period, consider waiting until the beginning of the next hiring period to turn in your application. You want your application to be noticed, not tossed onto a growing heap of last-minute paperwork.

Do not wait until the last minute to turn in your application. If you do this, not only will your application find its way to the bottom of the heap, it will be read by someone who has read hundreds or thousands of applications before getting to yours. Turning your application in well in advance of a deadline shows that you possess initiative and self-confidence, both of which are desirable qualities to display.

Follow Up if Possible

Most police departments have dedicated recruitment staff who are happy to answer inquiries from applicants. If you know where your application went, and if you know who read it, it is a good idea to call or e-mail with a short follow up, thanking that person for taking the time to read your application.

The reason for this is that the selection process can be gruelling for police recruiters, and selecting the right number of applicants to move forward in the process can be tough. There are many qualified candidates to consider, so putting in a little extra effort can really pay off in some cases.

In some cases, follow-up is discouraged. If there are specific instructions that advise candidates not to call or email recruitment staff, then follow those instructions.

In almost all cases, everyone who applies receives a response, either informing them that they have been selected for testing, or that their application has been rejected.

Be sure to follow these ten tips when writing your application. Take your time, think carefully about the questions and answer them truthfully. If your application is successful, you will be informed by the department you applied to with what comes next in the selection process. This will be the focus of the next chapter.

If your application is unfortunately unsuccessful, it may be worth contacting the department and asking for feedback. Ask what prevented your application from succeeding, and then try to focus on those weaknesses and make them your strengths for the next application. Don't give up – give it another go at a later date.

Chapter 4
Understanding the Selection Process

Congratulations on making it this far and having your application accepted. Unfortunately, you're not out of the woods yet – the selection process contains a number of stages.

Once a police department has accepted your application, you will go through a demanding selection process that includes written testing, physical testing, and assessment designed to determine whether you have the mental and emotional fortitude required to be an effective member of a law enforcement team.

It is vital that you learn as much as possible about tests prior to taking them, and it is also very important that you build yourself up physically in order to get great scores on physical aptitude tests. Not only will you be competing against perhaps hundreds of other applicants, you will be intentionally placed under increased stress so that recruiters may gauge the way you react when under pressure.

Watch your health carefully during this time. Ensure you exercise properly and eat right. Get plenty of rest, and abstain from substances that could detract from your performance; alcohol, while completely legal, is one substance you should consider staying away from while you are in the midst of the testing and selection process.

While most police agencies' tests vary somewhat from one to the next, many are quite similar. You will need to check the specifics with the department or departments you are applying to; however, the following information will help you understand more about some of the most common types of tests police candidates undergo during various portions of selection proceedings.

Written Tests

As previously mentioned, much of police work entails writing about details. Some police functions also involve mathematical equations. In addition, most police departments utilise a number of standardised forms. Written tests are designed to help police recruiters identify candidates who are capable of completing forms, performing simple mathematic equations, and writing cohesive sentences.

Most written tests of this kind include sections that cover reading comprehension, basic spelling and punctuation, basic science knowledge, some basic mathematics, and some short essay questions. Many departments and programs designed to aid police applicants through the selection process offer a selection of sample verbal reasoning tests, mathematical tests, and other tests as applicable.

It is very important to note that mechanical devices, such as calculators, are not normally allowed during testing. Neither are notes, cell phones, or other aids that could potentially skew a candidate's results. Most departments provide test materials, pencils, and scrap paper; nothing other than what is provided is normally allowed.

If it has been some time since you last took a written test, practising beforehand can be very helpful. Practice resources are easily available online and will help you discover your weaknesses, allowing you to turn them into your strengths for the actual test.

Remember that different police departments have slightly different tests, which may focus on different things. Make sure that you use the practice materials which match the departments that you are applying to.

Physical Aptitude and Agility Tests

Physical aptitude and agility tests are designed to ensure candidates are fit enough to begin rigorous physical training. While there are certain standards which must be met, it is a very good idea to ensure you can run faster, lift more weight, or complete certain activities better than the minimum requirements. All candidates are normally given complete information about what specific tests will consist of, well in advance of those tests being administered. In general, though, here are some very common aspects of physical testing:

• Running. Both short sprints and longer runs are usually part of physical aptitude testing. Distance and time varies from one department to the next.

- Physical Strength. There are a number of methods used to determine whether candidates possess the minimum physical strength requirements to successfully enter a police academy. These include grip strength tests, sit-ups, and push-ups; some departments may also have applicants demonstrate whether they are capable of lifting certain amounts of weight, or whether they are capable of dragging a heavy dummy for a certain distance.

- Agility Testing. Many departments require candidates to complete agility courses that include activities like climbing, crawling, and running, as well as carrying weight over a distance.

- Skin Fold Testing and Body Mass Indexing. Most departments will not hire a candidate or allow him or her to move forward with further testing if they are over-fat. Requirements vary from one department to the next.

- Eye Tests. Some departments do not require candidate sight testing; others administer simple eye tests to check for vision acuity and colour blindness.

Recruits must meet certain physical and medical standards because police academy and the jobs police officers do are, by nature, physically demanding. Police officers must have the stamina to safely deal with emergency situations, shift work, and everyday tasks.

Psychological Evaluation Tests

Psychological evaluation testing is sometimes administered concurrently with physical evaluation tests; however, this testing may also be administered at a separate site on a different date. Behavioural tests are designed to allow administrators to look for both positive and negative personal psychological aspects in order to select those candidates whom are best suited to employment within police departments. Various aspects of the tests focus on qualities such as:

- Integrity. Are you consistently honest with yourself and others? Would you be a positive role model for the community? Are you capable of setting aside self-interest when necessary?

- Leadership. Are you able to lead, guide, or influence other people by setting a positive example, using logic and facts, or delegating activities to others? Would you be an asset to a team? Can you accept personal accountability for your actions?

- Decisiveness. Are you capable of making speedy decisions based on the information available? Are you able to implement plans and focus under duress?

- Stress Management. Can you remain objective and solve problems under urgent time constraints or while managing rudeness, aggression, or danger?

- Compliance. Are you able to follow standard instructions, procedures, and routines in an environment that is governed by strictly outlined policies and procedures? Can you competently complete necessary documents in accordance with regulations?

- Problem Solving. Using job skills, judgment, and training, are you capable of gathering facts, determining options, and drawing sound, logical conclusions prior to implementing any action? How does personal emotion play a role in your problem solving skills? Do you suffer from anxiety that hinders astute problem solving?

- Flexibility. Can you find more than one way to solve a problem?

- Communication. Are you an effective verbal communicator? How well do you pick up on social cues? How are your interpersonal skills?

- Organisational Awareness. Are you capable of managing a number of complex tasks? How are your personal planning skills?

Some aspects of psychological testing will be verbally administered, and others may be given as written tests. For example, the Occupational Personality Questionnaire assesses candidates with respect to their capacity for coping with the responsibilities police officers face on a daily basis.

Interviews

There are a number of different types of interviews you may be submitted to during the selection process. These interviews often progress in difficulty. As you make your way through the process you may find yourself sitting or standing before a number of different police officials.

In some respects, these interviews are very much like other pre-employment interview proceedings you may have been through in the past. Interviews provide you with an opportunity to do more than just show officials why you are a quality candidate; they allow you to verbally explain why you are a good choice for the job. Further details about the interview, as well as how to prepare for it, will be provided in Chapters 6 and 7.

Background Checks

In today's world, no employer can be too careful; potential police recruits and other security personnel have traditionally been asked to submit to extensive background checks, and that is still true today.

Expect to fill out a very long questionnaire about all aspects of your personal life, your educational background, any questionable incidents you may have been involved in, and details regarding personal relationships.

The next chapter will discuss assessment centres, which you may be asked to attend during the selection process.

Chapter 5
How to Pass
the Assessment
Centre Tests

Attending an assessment centre is often part of the selection process, particularly if you are planning to apply to the AFP. If you must attend an assessment centre, prepare yourself for a long day by getting plenty of sleep the night before, and by taking good care of your health beforehand as well.

Be sure to get everything ready the day before you must leave to attend the Assessment Centre. You will be given a complete list of items to bring with you, which might include different documents and different types of clothing. Preparing in advance and double-checking everything on your list will ensure that you do not forget anything, and it will reduce your initial stress level. Be sure that you do not bring anything listed as "prohibited" to the test site with you.

A number of assessment techniques will be presented in a structured combination that allows for fairly quick, yet completely comprehensive assessment of each candidate. During the assessment process, you will very likely be interviewed, and you'll participate in written exercises. You may also participate in group discussions, along with individual presentations and psychological testing.

Once the Assessment Centre process has been completed, you will be advised of whether you are progressing to the next stage or not. If you are unsuccessful at Assessment Centre testing, you may reapply during the next intake period.

Whether you attend an Assessment Day or an Assessment Centre, or if your tests take place over a more extended period of time, it is very important to remember to relax, breathe easy, and just be the very best version of "you" you can be. The tests are specifically designed to physically, mentally, and emotionally elevate your stress levels so that officials can select the candidates who are best suited for the job of police officer. Reminding yourself of this fact can be helpful, and so can the following tips for each type of test.

Passing Written Tests

There are several ways to increase your chances of passing written police aptitude tests. The first and most important step is to find out what type of questions will be included on the test you are going to take. Most police departments provide specific information regarding what is on each section of every test. While they do not give hints about the exact questions that will be asked, they do provide quality samples that you can use to mentally prepare yourself.

For example, Victoria's Written Police Entrance Examination (PEE) consists of five separate types of tests:

• Language Comprehension and Spelling;

• English Skills;

• Writing;

• Reasoning Ability;

• Mathematics.

The South Australia Police Entry Exam is slightly different, consisting of six tests:

• Verbal Reasoning Ability;

• Non-verbal Reasoning Ability;

• Grammatical Knowledge;

• Reading Comprehension;

• Written Questions;

• Spelling.

If the police department you are applying to has a website, you can probably find and download a few sample questions there.

Some dedicated applicants find that taking police exam preparation courses is extremely helpful, and the majority of these people tend to do very well on the written portions of the exams. Of course, it is important to prepare for other types of testing as well since, in the end, you will be evaluated on merit of all the tests you took.

Success with Physical Aptitude and Agility Tests

In order to do well on physical aptitude and agility tests, you must be in good physical condition. If you will be taking the test in the same area you live in, and you train in that area, be sure to work out outdoors at least part of the time to simulate live conditions. If you will be taking the test at a higher altitude, then you should be prepared to encounter more difficulty with breathing, so exercise at a higher altitude whenever possible.

Remember that both your aerobic capacity and your level of actual physical strength will be tested, and keep in mind, your Body Mass Index (BMI) will be calculated with callipers. In general, there are three types of physical tests you must successfully complete.

Body Fat Skin Fold Test. In this test, skin callipers are used to measure four different anatomical locations where fat tends to accumulate. If you are a male, your body fat skin fold percentage should be 20% or less for a high score. A percentage of 20% to 23.9% is considered to be marginal, and men with body fat skin fold percentages greater than 23.9% do not pass.

Females should have a Body Mass Index of 30% or less for a perfect score. Scores between 30% and 33.9% are considered to be marginal, and scores of greater than 33.9% do not pass.

Multi-Stage Aerobic Fitness Tests. A common physical fitness test is the progressive 20-Metre Shuttle Run, in which all applicants are required to reach the standard of 50% as per Australia's fitness norms.

Sprints and Distance Runs. Sprint testing and distance running may or may not be included in the testing procedure for the department you test with. Focusing your workouts on both speed and endurance can help you succeed with these tests as well as with the 20 Metre Shuttle Run test.

Grip Strength, Pull-Ups, and Push-Ups. Depending on which

department you test with, you may be required to pass physical strength tests that focus on hand grip strength, abdominal strength, and upper body strength. Most police departments publish their test requirements; if you know that you will be required to take these tests, practise in advance so that you can easily exceed requirements rather than meet them with difficulty. Not practising can lead to abject failure, meaning that all the time you have spent preparing thus far has been completely wasted.

A sample Agility Test used by the South Australia Police is as follows:

Beginning inside a police vehicle, applicants must first climb over a 1-metre mesh fence, followed by a climb over a 1.5-metre colour bond fence. Following this, they must climb over a 3-metre cyclone fence, and then climb over a 1-metre wire fence. Next, each applicant must crawl through a small opening before leaping over a 1.5-metre ditch, then running through a simulated car park. After climbing over two 1-metre hurdles, each applicant must climb through a window. Next, a 25 kg simulated body must be dragged for a distance of 20 metres. The dummy is then dropped, and the applicant runs for 120 metres. Finally, a car wheel is removed from the boot of a police vehicle, carried to the front of the vehicle, and placed on the ground; the wheel is then lifted from the ground and carried back to the rear of the vehicle, where it is once again placed inside the vehicle's boot.

These tests are timed, and often, police recruitment personnel add to the stress by yelling at candidates as they make their attempts. While you may not be able to simulate each of these tests perfectly, practising running, climbing, crawling, and lifting heavy objects can make all the difference to your success.

By losing any excess weight and by placing yourself on a solid physical fitness regimen, you can pass these physical fitness tests with flying colours.

Doing Well on Psychological Tests

The best way to prepare for psychological testing is to prevent yourself from becoming too nervous about the whole procedure. Anyone who is of sound mind and who has an honest disposition tends to find that psychological testing is easy and even a bit fun.

Be completely honest as you answer written and verbal questions, and do not be surprised if you see the same questions a few times. This test is designed to help weed out anyone who is blatantly dishonest, or who is of questionable character. It is designed to help police recruitment officials look for signs of evasiveness, too.

Some of the questions you might be asked could involve asking you about certain situations that took place in the past. Be sure to provide honest answers, and be prepared to provide concrete evidence about the truthfulness of statements you provided. Do not succumb to the temptation to boast, and do not embellish anything, since some of these questions are designed specifically to provoke people who are prone to boasting or embellishment to slip up. Police officers must be honest. If you have trouble with honesty, work to improve your character before submitting to testing.

No matter what, be sure you are well rested and alert for your psychological evaluation. Try not to worry about what will take place; instead, just focus on providing truthful answers. Trying too hard to appear perfect will negatively impact your results, and can cause you to fail the test. The best way to pass a psychological test is to relax and be yourself.

Sample Questions

SAMPLE COMPETENCY BASED INTERVIEW QUESTION 1 (WORKING WITH OTHERS)

Please provide an example of where you have worked as part of a team to achieve a difficult task.

Tips for constructing your response:

• Try to think of a situation where you volunteered to work with a team in order to achieve a difficult task. It is better to say that you volunteered as opposed to being asked to get involved by another person.

• Those candidates who can provide an example where they achieved the task despite the constraints of time will generally score better.

• Consider structuring your response in the following manner:

STEP 1 Explain what the situation was and how you became involved.

STEP 2 Now explain who else was involved and what the task was.

STEP 3 Explain why the task was difficult and whether there were any time constraints.

STEP 4 Explain how it was decided who would carry out what task.

STEP 5 Now explain what had to be done and how you overcame any obstacles or hurdles.

STEP 6 Explain what the result/outcome was. Try to make the result positive as a result of your actions.

Now use the template on the following page to construct your own response to this question based on your own experiences and knowledge.

Sample competency based interview question 1

Please provide an example of where you have worked as part of a team to achieve a difficult task.

Examples of probing questions:

1. Would you have done anything different next time?

2. How did the end result make you feel?

SAMPLE COMPETENCY BASED INTERVIEW QUESTION 2 (PROFESSIONALISM)

Provide an example of where you have challenged someone's behavior that was either discriminatory or inappropriate. What did you do and what did you say?

Tips for constructing your response:

- Read carefully the core competency that relates to respect for race and diversity before constructing your response.

- When challenging this type of behavior, make sure you remain calm at all times and never become aggressive or confrontational.

- Consider structuring your response in the following manner:

STEP 1 Explain what the situation was and how you became involved.

STEP 2 Now explain who else was involved and why you felt that the behavior was inappropriate or discriminatory. What was it that was being said or done?

STEP 3 Now explain what you said or did and why.

STEP 4 Explain how the other person/people reacted when you challenged the behavior.

STEP 5 Now explain what the end result was. Try to make the result positive following your actions.

STEP 6 Finally, explain why you think it was that the people/ person behaved as they did.

Now use the template on the following page to construct your own response to this question based on your own experiences and knowledge.

Sample competency based interview question 2

Provide an example of where you have challenged someone's behavior that was either discriminatory or inappropriate. What did you do and what did you say?

Examples of probing questions:

1. How did you feel when you were challenging their behavior?

2. How did the person or people react when you challenged their behavior?

SAMPLE COMPETENCY BASED INTERVIEW QUESTION 3 (WORKING WITH OTHERS)

Provide an example of where you have helped somebody from a different culture or background to your own. What did you do and what did you say?

Tips for constructing your response:

- Read carefully the core competency that relates to respect for race and diversity before constructing your response.

- Try to think of a situation where you have gone out of your way to help somebody.

- Try to use keywords and phrases from the core competency in your response.

Consider structuring your response in the following manner:

STEP 1 Explain what the situation was and how you became involved. It is better to say that you volunteered to be involved rather than to say that you were asked to.

STEP 2 Now explain who else was involved and why they needed your help or assistance?

STEP 3 Now explain what you said or did and why. Also explain any factors you took into consideration when helping them.

STEP 4 Explain how the other person/people reacted to your help or assistance. Did they benefit from it?

STEP 5 Now explain what the end result was. Try to make the result positive following your actions.

Now use the template on the following page to construct your own response to this question based on your own experiences and knowledge.

Sample competency based interview question 3

Provide an example of where you have helped somebody from a different culture or background to your own. What did you do and what did you say?

Examples of probing questions:

1.   What did you learn from this experience?

2.   Would you have done anything differently?

If you pass the tests at the assessment centre, you will likely be called for an interview. Details on how the interview proceeds, as well as tips on how to pass it, are provided in the following two chapters.

Chapter 6
Preparing for the Interview

As mentioned previously, police applicants must often present themselves to be interviewed several times during the selection process. This can be something to be enjoyed, or it may be completely nerve-wracking; depending on your personality, you might feel frightened or eager prior to interviews. There are several ways you can prepare yourself in advance: physically, mentally, and emotionally.

The Interview

Generally speaking, the interview is conducted by a panel of police officers, recruiters, and members of the community. The number of interviewers on the panel may vary between departments as well as their position in the police service or the community. Each department's website should provide information on the interview, including who the panel consists of.

Make sure that you are aware of what kind of questions the panel will ask you, as specifics may differ between departments. By doing this, you will prevent yourself from being caught off-guard. Bear in mind that the role of the interview is not to catch you out or give you trick questions. If you've made it this far, then the recruiters are clearly impressed with your performance. The interview is used to verify what they've seen in written and verbal tests, as well as develop an understanding of you as a person.

Appearance

It may go without saying, but your appearance is just as important to your success when interviewing for a position on a police force as it is when applying for any other type of job. You want to look professional, mature, and responsible, so be sure to follow any instructions you are given when you are advised of your interview date. Some departments intentionally provide no guidelines for applicants to follow, since they want to see whether applicants possess the maturity to dress properly for an interview. Here are some general guidelines for putting your best foot forward.

If you do not currently wear a conservative hairstyle, now is the time to make an appointment for a haircut. Men should generally wear their hair short, although religious headwear is also allowed.

Women should either opt for a short haircut, no longer than collar-length, or plan to wear their hair up during all interviews and tests. Your hair colour should be natural; if you consistently dye your hair a very different colour than the colour it is naturally, consider allowing it to return to a more natural shade. When you reach the police academy, you will be expected to maintain a simple hairstyle that looks professional. If you have very long hair, consider the fact that people can easily grab it and use it as a method for hurting you. In the police academy setting, instructors do all they can to simulate real-world situations, so keep this in mind when deciding on a hairstyle.

For interviews and other pre-employment screening, men should not wear earrings; if you wear earrings now, consider removing them and allowing the holes to close for a more professional appearance.

Women should wear conservative earring styles for police interviews; very small hoops or studs are usually considered to be appropriate.

Necklaces may be worn, but they should be simple and conservative as well; any rings other than engagement rings or wedding bands should be removed prior to the interview.

Facial piercings of any kind should be removed well before the interview. You will not normally be allowed to keep a facial piercing in place while you are in the police academy, nor are you likely to be allowed to retain a facial piercing while employed by a police department.

Men should not wear makeup of any kind to a police interview, and women should aim for a natural look. Light cologne is normally acceptable, but do not drench yourself in it. Remember that you are trying to become a police officer, not attract a mate.

If you don't have a wristwatch, consider getting one that is conservatively styled and functional. Police officers must keep close track of the time, and wearing a good wristwatch to a law enforcement interview can help to support the responsible image that you are aiming for.

For men, a suit and tie is never a poor choice. Women should aim for professional-looking attire; if you elect to wear a skirt, be sure it hits you right at the knees. Too long or too short may come across as unprofessional.

If you do not have a suit and cannot afford to buy one, put together as professional a look as you possibly can. Under no circumstances should you wear shorts, t-shirts, tank tops or other sleeveless styles, jeans, baggy trousers, tennis shoes, shoes with very high heels, or any type of sandals to a police interview. Look for styles that are professional and not too trendy - aim for a classic business look and you should make a good impression.

Whatever you wear, be sure that it is clean and well pressed. Ensure that your shoes are clean and free of scuffmarks. If the material they are made from is meant to be shiny, then shine your shoes the night before the interview so that they will be dry and gleaming in the morning. Do not wear your jacket while driving or riding to the interview, since doing so can give you a rumpled appearance.

Arrive at your destination a few minutes early, and put on your jacket before entering the building. When you arrive, try to visit the washroom before waiting for your interview. Take a quick peek in the mirror to ensure that your wardrobe is not malfunctioning in any way.

Personal hygiene is another issue that some candidates have an issue with. Ensure you are freshly showered, and completely clean from head to toe before heading out for your interview. Use mouthwash, brush and floss your teeth, and freshen your breath again a few minutes before the interview is slated to begin. Do this privately, not in front of office staff. Using appropriate deodorants, antiperspirants, and other hygienic products is an important part of public life.

No matter what, remember that the first impression people receive when they first see you is completely up to you. Presenting a positive appearance is the first step to interview success.

Personal Presentation

Whilst your clothing, hairstyle and general appearance affect the quality of the impression you make, so does the way you present yourself as you encounter various people before, during, and after the interview.

If you drive to the interview, be sure to wash your car first. Often, interviewers and other personnel look out from windows to see the way candidates approach, and arriving in a filthy vehicle is definitely not going to score any points in your favour. If there is a guarded gate, be sure to be friendly with the gate guard, and greet any office staff, such as a front desk receptionist, with a friendly attitude as well.

No matter what you do, mind your posture. The goal here is to present yourself in as confident and self-assured manner possible. Even if you find yourself waiting for a long while, don't slouch in your chair or lean against walls. It is okay to relax a bit if you are in a lounge area, but keep in mind, people are watching and will probably be asked about the impression you made on them.

Avoid playing games and surfing the Internet on your mobile phone while waiting for your interview, and before the interview begins, be sure to turn the volume completely off, unless there is some kind of emergency you are dealing with. In this case, you should place the phone on vibrate and excuse yourself in advance for expecting a call that you cannot wait for.

Make eye contact with people you meet, and be sure to greet your interviewers with a firm and confident handshake. If you're new at shaking hands with people, consider getting a friend to practise with you so that you can perfect your grip.

Before the interview, you may have the opportunity to speak on the telephone with some of the people with whom you will be coming into contact. Remember, talking on the phone with a potential employer is much different from chatting with a friend. Do not allow any distractions to interfere; if you pick up the phone while TV or radio noise is happening in the background, excuse yourself while you shut off the volume. Be professional with the words you use, and if you need to, take a few notes about the content of the conversation.

You might be surprised at the impressions a few minutes on the telephone can make with a potential interviewer. In addition, even if the person you speak with is not the same person who will be interviewing you later, he or she is almost certain to relay any impressions, positive or negative, to the person or people who will be conducting interviews.

Now is a good time to address the content of your voice mail or answering machine message, too. If you think there is even a remote chance that someone from a department you are applying with is going to call you on the telephone, assess the quality of the message that the person may hear in the event you do not pick up. If you have provided a telephone number to a potential employer, this applies to you!

The best course of action is to have a simple, straightforward recording:

"Hello, you have reached (your name) at (your complete telephone number). I cannot come to the phone right now. Please leave a detailed message and I will call you back as soon as possible."

If you use ringback tones on your mobile phone, and that is the phone number you have provided officials with, then carefully consider the way that your choice of music may affect your chances of making the right kind of impression. Instead of taking chances, you may want to abandon your ringback tone for the time being, and simply choose a simple, standard ring to be on the safe side.

Mental and Emotional Preparation

Being mentally and emotionally prepared to deal with the rigors associated with the interview process is just as important as being able to physically prepare yourself. If you have interviewed for jobs or other positions in the past, you definitely have a bit of an advantage over young people who have never been interviewed, and if you have taken advantage of police preparation courses, you might be at an even greater advantage, particularly if those courses included practice interviews. Whatever the case, almost everyone hoping to gain employment as a police officer suffers some mental and emotional distress before, during, and after interviews.

To combat this, it is important that you put things in their proper perspective, and really prepare yourself for whatever might happen during the interview. Along the way, it is important to remind yourself of the following:

- Police interviewers are people, too.

- The officers and other officials who interview you were once beginners like you.

- The department you are interviewing with is conducting interviews because the need for police officers is present. The interviewer's objective is to find suitable candidates for the job at hand, not to interrogate criminal suspects.

- Making mistakes during a high-stress interview is something that a lot of people do. Whilst not desirable, it does happen frequently and you shouldn't worry yourself too much about it.

- How you say things is just as important as what you say. Pause to think for a moment before giving an answer; this also buys you some time to take a breath and relax a little before responding to questions.

One of the best ways to beat interview stress is to ensure that you are completely prepared for your interview, well in advance of the date that it actually occurs. One of the best ways to do this is to assemble a collection of common interview questions and prepare answers in the event those questions are asked. If you have ever had to give any kind of performance, then you probably know just how important rehearsal is.

Once you have prepared yourself somewhat, enlist a trusted friend or family member to help you practise. Whilst doing this, it is a good idea to keep the basic content of your answers the same, while varying your response slightly, so that when the day of your interview arrives, you will not sound overly rehearsed.

In the next chapter, we will review several common police interview questions and answers; you should be sure to go over those carefully, and you should take the time to learn more about the police department or departments you are applying to, as well; in many cases, you will be asked questions that directly relate to specific areas.

Learning more about specific departments, including their histories, geographic areas they serve, and public service programs and departmental policies can help you make a better impression, plus it can help you feel a bit more at ease during your interview. Think of it this way - the better you know someone, the easier it is to talk to him or her. Since your interviewer is a representative of the department you are interviewing with, your knowledge will give you something in common.

At the same time, it is very important not to come off as a know-it-all. Whilst confidence is extremely important, overconfidence and bragging are not viewed as positive attributes. Keeping a sense of humility and displaying a willingness to learn are, on the other hand, two good ways to provide interviewers with a positive impression of your attitude.

As you prepare your mind for the initial interview and additional interviews that are likely to follow in the event you make it past initial testing, you should know that police employment interviews are often panel interviews, in which two or more individuals from the department interview candidates for employment. There are several reasons for this.

Panel interviews are, by nature, somewhat more intimidating than standard interviews with only one interviewer present. Placing you under pressure allows interviewers to more accurately judge your aptitude for police work; but, they also provide you with an advantage by ensuring that more than one person gets the chance to receive a first impression from you, listen to your answers, and form an overall opinion of you. After panel interviews conclude, interviewers invariably discuss the candidates they have seen; this can also help since people with different personalities contribute to decisions regarding the next stage of the hiring process.

In case you've heard that police departments use panel interviews as an intimidation tactic, you should be aware that not everything you hear about these interviews is true. While that may have been the case in the past, today's police departments are often all about teamwork.

The panel interview increases the speed with which interviews can be undertaken, plus it makes for greater accuracy. In many cases, subordinate officers get to participate in panel interviews, allowing candidates to make an impression on some of the people they may one day end up working alongside. In addition, panel interviews allow more people to ask for clarification; when only a single person is interviewing you, you only get the opportunity to have that person take the initiative to ask you to expand upon the answers you are giving.

Finally, it is a well-known fact that when panel interviews are conducted properly, they deliver better quality in terms of results. Fewer hiring mistakes are made, and candidates chosen after panel interviews have concluded tend to make excellent additions to the police department.

With panel interviews, don't be surprised if one interviewer does much of the talking, while other members of the interviewing panel sit quietly and observe, without contributing very much at all. Often, other interviewers will interject, and in some cases, interviewers may take turns asking questions. Whatever the case may be, do not take it personally. Do your best to stay calm and relaxed. Often, police employment interviews are scheduled to take place over just a few days, one after another. Interviewers often take turns talking and listening, just to make their workload a little bit lighter.

Depending on what part of the hiring process you are in, an interview could last for only a few minutes, or it could take longer than an hour. In either case, be sure that you have prepared by ensuring you are as rested as possible beforehand.

Most people find that the better prepared they are for an interview, the less they worry about it beforehand, and that's a good thing. The less stress you show under pressure, the better. If you are not well prepared, you might try to make up for it by mentally rehearsing questions and answers right before the interview, a mistake that you might be familiar with if you have ever faced any kind of test less prepared than you would like to be. Research has shown time and again that cramming just does not work. Do yourself a huge favour, and start preparing now, even if you have no interviews lined up at present.

Finally, let's take a moment to talk about the way in which you speak. If you have spent any time in the public eye, than you probably have developed a good sense of what kind of speech is appropriate, and what kind of speech should be avoided any time you are talking with someone other than a friend or a family member. If you have ever taken public speaking classes, some of what you learned there can help you as well.

If you are brand new to being interviewed or speaking in front of a group of a few people who are hanging on your every word, then pay very close attention to the way that you speak, and do your best to remedy any problems that arise before you ever reach the inner sanctum of the police department's interview room. Here are a few helpful hints to help prevent you from feeling as though you need to put your foot in your mouth in the middle of an interview:

- Stop using slang. Work on enunciating each word you speak.

- Make room for pauses within your speech, if you have a tendency to speak rapidly. If you have a tendency to speak very slowly and pause frequently to think while you are speaking, work on speeding up slightly. Whether you speak slowly or quickly as a rule, your speech pattern will intensify if you are feeling stressed.

- Think about the way in which you tend to form your sentences. Does the way you speak make sense, or are people sometimes confused because you meander from one subject to the next, eventually coming to a conclusion after explaining things in a roundabout way? If you are not sure about this, ask someone you trust for an honest evaluation. If someone gives you good advice, be sure to take it and put it into use.

- Watch out for "um" and "uh". Even though some heads of state, news broadcasters, and other speakers suffer from an occasional bout of stuttering, excessive stammering can place you at a severe disadvantage. If you commonly express confusion aloud by using expressions like these, do your best to limit any speech patterns that interviewers might interpret as nervousness or unpreparedness.

- If you are completely awkward with speaking in front of anyone, consider joining a group like Toastmasters International, or think about taking a course in public speaking. Make a habit of speaking to as many strangers as you can, as often as possible. If you want to be a police officer, you are going to have to learn how to express yourself with confidence and authority.

In addition to following these tips regarding the way in which you speak, consider the way your body language works. Body language often belies nervousness or insecurity, and police interviewers are masters at interpreting it. Aim for a natural, confident manner of speaking, and avoid making nervous movements while you are speaking.

People who are nervous often do not make normal hand gestures while speaking; others rehearse hand gestures to the point of ridiculousness. You might not really be aware of the way your own hand gestures look, so consider having your practice interviews recorded to find out what you look like while you are interviewing.

A person who is confident while being interviewed often appears slightly relaxed, yet he or she never slouches. When explaining details, hand gestures often come into play; they too look natural, unforced, and not the least bit nervous.

Some common problems with body language include obvious nervous habits, like nail biting, chewing on the lips or licking the lips, or tapping the feet in an unsettled manner. If these habits sound familiar to you, watch out for them so you can stop them before they become a problem.

Some people have a habit of clasping their hands tightly together when nervous, while others fold their arms across their chests. Some make darting or apparently furtive eye motions, while others can't seem to stop fiddling with their clothing. Others shift nervously in their seats, and some constantly touch their hair or their faces.

Knowing which nervous habits you are susceptible to, and training yourself not to display them, can give you an enormous edge over the competition. All of your competitors are bound to be just as nervous as you are, but most of whom will probably not be well prepared to deal with the kind of nervous behaviour that acts just like a glowing neon sign, telling interviewers just how ill at ease they are.

The 'Dos' and 'Don'ts' of Interpersonal Communications

Now that we've talked about you and the way that you present yourself, let's take a look at some important strategies for making the most of interpersonal communications. If you've had the opportunity to spend any amount of time in the workforce, then you probably know many of these rules already. If you have taken jobs training courses then you may be aware of them as well. However, it never hurts to make a review of helpful information, particularly when your future is involved.

Do your best to learn the names and titles of the people who will be interviewing you. In some cases, you may have met the investigating officers in the past, and you may be familiar with them. If this is true, then greet the people you know by name as you shake their hands; even if you know their first names, use their titles, followed by their surnames. For example, as you're shaking hands with Officer Joe Smith, make eye contact and say "Good Afternoon, Officer Smith." Tailor your greetings to suit the situation.

If people are being introduced to you and you are greeting them, do your best to memorize their names, and when you leave, thank them personally. By using names and titles you not only show respect, but you also provide the interviewers with the impression that you are mature and comfortable in professional situations.

It is very helpful to learn how to identify communication styles and tailor your own communication to match with the style interviewer's display to some extent. This is similar to a process called mirroring, in which people either consciously or unconsciously imitate certain aspects of another person's body language whilst involved in communication.

Often, when this behaviour is displayed, certain miming gestures may be used; these can include breathing tempo, accent, attitude, eye movements, and even choice of words. Using mirroring techniques can help the person you are conversing with feel more open to you.

Increasing synchronicity in this manner can make the interview process feel smoother, but any mirroring should look and feel natural or it will act against you rather than aiding the communications process. Watch yourself for mirroring in everyday conversation and see how it works; it is a technique master communicators use with skill and great success, and it is not difficult to learn.

Another important aspect of interpersonal communications in regard to interviewing is active listening. While you do not want to paraphrase questions that are posed to you or repeat them verbatim, you do want to address the questions carefully, showing that you heard them correctly; do not be too embarrassed to ask for clarification if a question is not clear. This does not make you look foolish; in fact, it shows that you are paying close attention to the questions being asked, and it proves that you take a thoughtful approach to the act of listening and responding to questions.

Practise communicating as often as possible, and consider taking classes if you are ill at ease in interview situations. The more confident and self-assured you are, the better your interview will go.

In the next chapter, you will have the opportunity to read some sample interview questions. Take note of the sample answers and tailor them to suit your personality and experiences.

Chapter 7
Sample
Interview
Questions and
Answers

If you have ever been in the position of being interviewed, or if you have interviewed others in the past, then you will probably be familiar with some of these questions. Interestingly, many of the questions posed to people applying to be police officers are similar to those asked of candidates for other jobs.

Some of the questions you will be asked may make you feel a bit uncomfortable, as they may be extremely personal in nature. It is advisable never to lie about anything, and it is also advisable to openly admit mistakes you have made in the past. You are applying for a position in which you will be required to uphold the law. Do not give in to the temptation to embellish answers or bend the truth, even a little bit.

In this chapter, we will cover both types of questions, and you will learn some methods for answering them. Remember, you will need to tailor your responses to suit your own situation. In addition, not all departments use the same questions.

Probing Questions

Probing questions are designed to allow the interviewers to learn more about you. There are several different areas that may be covered during this phase of the interview, and questions may be asked in any order. The following questions are commonly asked.

What do you know about this department?
This is your opportunity to show how much you know about the department you are applying for. If you go into the interview not knowing anything about the department you are applying for, you'll begin to look like a poor candidate for the position. Prepare yourself for this question, but don't feel pressured to know everything.

Why do you want a career in law enforcement?
Your interviewers really do want to know why you want a career like this. If you have wanted to be a police officer since you were a little kid, tell them that. Tell the interviewers why you find the opportunity attractive. Maybe you think you would be a good investigator; or, perhaps you want to protect your community. One strategy that

never works here is to tell your interviewing panel that you want to make arrests and beat up bad guys; this is guaranteed to make you look like a potential liability to the department.

Why do you want a job with this department?

The interviewers may ask this question. You should understand that flattery will get you nowhere; instead, tell them what you like about the agency. If you have heard positive statements about the agency, then tell them what you have heard. If you know someone who works there who is a positive role model, it's fine to use that person's name. Be honest, but don't go overboard.

Have you applied to any other law enforcement agencies?

Don't be afraid to answer this question honestly. Most candidates apply to every law enforcement agency that they are interested in. Tell them what agencies you have applied with, and if they ask you what your hiring status is with other agencies, be honest. Applying to many agencies at once is not a negative factor at all; it simply proves your determination to get into law enforcement.

Tell us about your goals.

Use this question as an opportunity to talk about your goals, as far as police work is concerned. If you are interested in working on a narcotics task force or becoming a homicide detective, now is the time to say so. This question gives interviewers the opportunity to see that you are a good candidate.

Which of your qualities would make you a good police officer?

This question might be posed as "What are your strong points," or perhaps as "What assets could you provide to this agency?" This is a good chance for you to brag a little about the good qualities you possess. Remember, there is a difference between articulating your strengths and shameless boasting. Be frank and state your strengths as factors that are measurable or documented in some way. Be prepared for this question, as it is one that is asked almost without fail.

What are your weaknesses?

Admitting that there are areas in which you need improvement is not a bad thing, and a candidate who can find no weaknesses within himself or herself could end up looking like a braggart. Pick one or two weaknesses in advance, and start working to improve them. Talk about the steps you are taking to improve yourself as you describe your weaknesses.

What duties did you perform at your previous (or current) place of employment?

Do your best to show that you are a dependable worker who is capable of getting the job done. If you have been a supervisor at any point, be sure to mention that. Don't use this as an opportunity to complain about job requirements you dislike. Talk about the positives.

Why did you leave your last job (or any job)?

Be truthful. If you left one job for another that was more appealing in some way, say so. If you were fired, be honest about it, but be sure to mention what you learned from the incident.

Have you ever been involved in an accident or been issued a traffic citation?

Your interviewers probably already know the answer to this question. They are looking for honesty, so be sure to tell the truth. It is a good idea to review your driving history before your interview so that you don't omit anything by accident.

Have you ever been arrested?

Again, this is a question that interviewers will probably have the answer to and, again, this is an opportunity to prove your trustworthiness by telling the truth. You will probably be asked for details about the case. Be honest, and talk about lessons learned.

Have you ever used (or sold) illegal drugs?

Again, be honest. The interviewers are looking for patterns. If you tried marijuana as a teenager, say so. If you had a drug habit, you should be open about it. Remember, police officers understand that people are capable of reforming themselves. Do not give in to the temptation to lie about drug activity.

Do you drink alcohol?
Drinking alcohol is common in our society, and it is legal. If you drink alcohol, say so. You will probably be asked about your drinking habits; again, be honest. If you had a tendency to party while you were in college and later you cleaned up your act, be truthful. If you do not drink alcohol, explain why not.

How is your credit?
If you are in financial debt of some kind, say so. Most people have credit card balances, car payments, mortgages, and so forth. With this question, interviewers are looking for insight into your dependability. If your debt situation is out of control right now, do all you can to improve it before your interview. Often, people with out of control spending habits and poor debt repayment habits are viewed as liabilities since they are often less dependable than those with good spending and repayment habits.

Do you have any medical problems that would prevent you from performing police duties as assigned?
Questions about your health are normal. You might be asked about past or present illnesses, medications you take or have taken in the past, and surgeries you may have had. Police officers need to be physically sound, and they need to possess good vision, too. If you are not physically fit right now, do all you can to get yourself into shape and improve your health well in advance of potential interviews.

Are you willing to submit to a (medical, psychological, fitness, or drug) test?
The answer here is "yes". If you want to be a police officer, you need to be drug free, physically fit, healthy, and in a strong psychological state. All interviewers need is your assent. If you say "no" then be prepared for questions about why you are not open to testing.

Verifying Questions

Verifying questions are intended to confirm that the data you have already submitted is factual. These questions are very easy to answer; usually, they are the same questions you have already answered on various forms.

Be prepared to answer questions about your current address and previous addresses, and discuss the reason for any moves you might have made. If you were ever evicted from a residence, be prepared to answer for it honestly.

Questions about your schooling will probably arise, too. You should be sure to go over old school records before your interview, just to be sure your memory is refreshed. Be prepared to talk about scores you received, disciplinary action that may have been taken against you, and any honours you might have received during the course of your schooling.

Your employment history might come up again here. At this point, interviewers are simply trying to verify facts.

Hypothetical Questions

Hypothetical questions cannot be answered with a simple yes or no; instead, you will be asked to explain how or why you would or would not do certain things. There are many different scenarios that might arise, and in some cases, a dilemma of wanting to do two things at once might exist. In any case, the goal here is to choose the most appropriate course of action.

No matter what questions are asked, take a moment to think about your answer before speaking instead of blurting out the first idea that enters your mind. In this case, a well thought out answer and a solid response is much more important than a lightning fast response; be careful though, taking too long to think could affect your rating.

Once you have provided an answer, expect to be asked to justify why you chose the course of action you did. In addition, be prepared to be asked why you did not do something. This does not mean that the answers you provided were wrong; analysis is a normal part of the hypothetical question phase. If you know you gave a good answer, stick to your guns.

Hypothetical questions are normally designed to allow interviewers to evaluate the way you would perform in specific areas such as judgment, integrity, use of force, dealing with co-workers, or supervising other people. A good way to prepare for these questions is to learn about standard law enforcement policies - often, departments publish information about their policies online. If you have the opportunity to prepare yourself for a career in law enforcement by taking classes of any kind, you can be assured that hypothetical questions and various scenarios will be discussed at length, giving you an even better idea about the role of a police officer and providing you with valuable food for thought.

Sample Questions and Answers

Use the following sample questions and exemplary answers to get an understanding of how the information provided to you in this chapter can be applied to real questions.

SAMPLE QUESTION NUMBER 1

"Tell us why you want to become a police officer."

Sample Response

"I have worked in my current role now for a number of years. I have an excellent employer and enjoy working for them but unfortunately no longer find my job challenging. I understand that the role of a police officer is both demanding and rewarding and I believe I have the qualities to thrive in such an environment. I love working under pressure, working as part of a team that is diverse in nature and helping people in difficult situations. The public expectations of the police are very high and I believe I have the right qualities to help the police deliver the right service to the community. I have studied the police core competencies and believe that I have the skills to match them and deliver what they require."

Top Tips

• Don't be negative about your current or previous employer.

- Be positive, enthusiastic and upbeat in your response.
- Make reference to the core competencies if possible.

SAMPLE QUESTION NUMBER 2

"Why have you chosen this particular Police Service?"

Sample Response

"I have carried out extensive research into the Police Service and in particular this constabulary. I have been impressed by the level of service it provides. The website provides the community with direct access to a different range of topics and the work that is being carried out through your community wardens is impressive. I have looked at the national and local crime statistics and read many different newspapers and articles. I like this Police Service because of its reputation and the police officers that I have spoken to have told me that they get a great deal of job satisfaction from working here."

Top Tips

- Research the service thoroughly and make reference to particular success stories that they have achieved.
- Be positive, enthusiastic and upbeat in your response.
- Be positive about their service and don't be critical of it, even if you think it needs improving in certain areas.

SAMPLE QUESTION NUMBER 3

"What does the role of a police officer involve?"

Sample Response

"Before I carried out my research and looked into the role of the police officer, I had the normal, stereotypical view of a police officer in that they catch criminals and reduce crime for a living. Whilst there is an element

of that in the job, the police officer's role is far more diverse and varied. For example, they are there to serve the community and reduce the element of fear. They do this by communicating with their communities and being visual wherever possible. They may need to pay particular attention to a person or groups of people who are the victims of crime or hatred. Therefore the role of a police officer is to both physically and psychologically protect the community that they are serving. It is also their role to work with other organizations such as the Fire Service, Social Services and other public sector bodies to try to reduce crime in a coordinated response as opposed to on their own."

Top Tips

• Understand the police core competencies and be able to recite them word for word.

SAMPLE QUESTION NUMBER 4

"If one of the members of your team was gay and they told you this over a cup of tea at work, how do you think you would react?"

Sample Response

"I would have no problem at all. A person's sexual preference is their right and they should not be treated any differently for this. My attitude towards them and our working relationship would not be affected in any way. I have always treated everyone with respect and dignity at all times and will continue to do so throughout my career."

Top Tips

• Understand everything there is to know about equality and fairness. If you do not believe in it then this job is not for you.

Chapter 8
Useful Contact
Information

What if you know that you would like to be a police officer, but you have no clue about how to get started? The following information can help you get a start in law enforcement. Here, you will find a number of valuable Internet sites, telephone numbers, and other information for finding employment with a police agency in Australia.

Australian Law Enforcement Agency Information

Australian Federal Police
For information on jobs with the AFP, go to http://www.afp.gov.au/jobs.aspx

All applications for employment with AFP must be lodged online. There are a number of downloadable pamphlets available on the site that provide detailed information about the job openings available with the Australian Federal Police.

In addition, the website provides detailed information regarding requirements and it discusses the hiring process in detail, including information about the Assessment Centre.

New South Wales Police
Visit http://www.police.nsw.gov.au/recruitment for in-depth information about jobs with the New South Wales Police.

The website includes a number of videos with details about various jobs within the police department, as well as a number of informational pages full of helpful discussion regarding the hiring process and the requirements you need to pass to apply to join the NSW Police Force.

If you wish to speak to a recruiter, you should call 1800 222 122

For information about the Associate Degree in Policing Practice offered by Charles Sturt University Admissions Centre, call 1800 443 306, or go to:

http://www.csu.edu.au/study/arts-courses/policing/

You can get information about the Bachelor of Policing offered by the University of Western Sydney at 1800 897 669, or visit:

http://myfuture.uws.edu.au/future_students_home/ug/policing_and_criminology/bachelor_of_policing

Northern Territory Police, Fire and Emergency Services
To obtain information about becoming a police officer with the Northern Territory Police, visit:

http://www.pfes.nt.gov.au/Police/Careers-in-policing/Constable.aspx

On the website, you will find detailed information about requirements, as well as details about Assessment Centres, including dates when they are held. You may also submit an application online.

If you have questions about a Northern Territory Constable application, you may call the recruitment office at 1800 005 099.

Queensland Police
To speak with a recruiter with the Queensland Police department, call 1300 Be A Cop or visit the police department's recruitment page for plenty of helpful information about employment, academy life, and much more. Requirements and general entry application is available at:

http://www.policerecruit.qld.gov.au/

South Australia Police
There are several employment opportunities available within the South Australian Police Force. Whether you want to become a police officer, a community constable, or a protective security officer, you can find detailed information as well as applications and requirements at:

http://www.achievemore.com.au/

Explore this site for information about available recruitment seminars and upcoming tests. There are special sections available for UK and New Zealand applicants.

Tasmania Police

Learn about eligibility requirements and find detailed information about the Tasmania Police by visiting the forces' website at:

http://www.police.tas.gov.au/join-us/

Online applications are available, as are details about the recruitment process and Trainee Constable Courses.

Western Australia Police

The Western Australia Police force offers a number of different career paths to parties interested in joining the department. The best way to learn about available openings is to visit the agency's website at:

http://www.stepforward.wa.gov.au/

Here, you will find comprehensive information including eligibility requirements, practice tests, helpful information for preparing yourself for the Assessment Centres, and much more. You may also submit an application for employment online.

If you would like to speak to recruitment personnel, you may call (08) 9301 9607.

Victoria

For information about serving in Victoria's police department, visit their website at:

http://www.policecareer.vic.gov.au/

You will find detailed information regarding career paths and other valuable information including requirements and online applications.

Pre-Employment Education

One of the best ways to prepare yourself for the rigors of police academy life, and a fantastic way to get a leg up on the competition, law enforcement education is available at a number of schools in Australia.

Some police agencies offer special cadet programs for teens who are interested in taking up a career in policing; if you are under 18, you may qualify to participate in one of these special opportunities. Check with the websites listed above to see whether opportunities are available in your area, or visit your local police station to find out if educational opportunities exist.

Australian Graduate School of Policing

Established in 1993, the Australian Graduate School of Policing (AGSP) is recognised globally as a leading provider of postgraduate research and education for those who wish to excel in the field of professional law enforcement. Offering courses in enforcement, emergency management, security and more, the school is staffed by professionals from every area of those fields.

For more information, visit:

www.csu.edu.au/faculty/arts/agsp/

University of Tasmania

Offering Graduate Certificates, Graduate Diplomas and Master Degrees in police studies, the University of Tasmania's police studies program features a number of courses designed to provide students with thorough grounding in policing theory and practice, as well as the skills needed to understand the field as a whole. Criminology theory and practice courses are also available; be sure to check with the university for current course catalogue offerings.

Programs are available on site at Hobart, with distance and flexible learning opportunities as well.

Visit:

http://www.postgraduate.utas.edu.au/all-faculties-and-institutes/

courses/faculty-of-arts2/police-studies

Victoria University

An approved testing centre for the Victoria Police Education Entrane Examination, offering testing that meets the first of several phases of the Victoria Police Recruiting process, Victoria University is the first stop for anyone who wishes to join the Victoria Police force.

In order to lodge an application with Victoria Police, you must first successfully complete all components of the examination.

To register for this course, you must go to:

http://www.vu.edu.au/courses/victoria-police-entrance-examination-vnpole

Follow the instructions at the bottom of the page. There, you will find a downloadable form that you can print and complete. When finished, submit the form to:

Police Program Coordinator
Victoria University Community Initiatives Program (VUCIP)
Victoria University
PO Box 14428 Melbourne VIC 8001
Ph: 03 9919 8714 Fax: 03 9919 8516
Email: policeprogram@vu.edu.au

On the page, you'll find detailed information about examination dates as well as details regarding information covered on exams. Registrations close fourteen days prior to examination dates, and must be paid in full to secure a place.

Conclusion

As you make your way forward toward an eventual career as an Australian police officer, try not to rush things. Rushing can cause you to skip important steps, and trying to prepare too fast will not be as effective as taking the time to carefully prepare will.

In addition, be sure not to procrastinate if there are areas in which you need improvement. Even someone police agencies consider to be a great candidate can make improvements upon himself or herself - there is always room to improve; no matter how well educated or well-rounded a person you are.

Make time for physical fitness each day, before you even think about attending an Assessment Centre. By working toward greater fitness, you improve the likelihood that you will pass all physical fitness tests. In addition, new cadets who are physically fit have a much easier time with all aspects of academy life. Do yourself a favour and start working out now. Focus on both aerobic capacity and muscular strength, and do your best to make healthy choices in various areas of your daily life.

By making a few changes to your daily routine, and by working to prepare yourself well in advance, you'll provide yourself with an advantage over the competition. Before you know it, you could be wearing a police uniform with pride.

For more help with the Police Officer tests see our other workbook:

www.HOW2BECOME.com